Secure

SCHOOL OF THE WORD

Titles in the School of the Word series:

A Life of Worship	John Johnson & Mike Stevens
According to Your Faith	Bryn Jones
Battle for the Mind	Stephen Matthew
Be Eager to Prophesy	Hugh Thompson
Called to be a Disciple	Dale Barnes
Christian Manhood	David Matthew
Effective Prayer	Bryn Jones
Essential Foundations	Hugh Thompson
Excelling as a Woman	Barbie Reynolds
Fulfilment in Marriage	Hugh & Rosemary Thompson
Go and Make Disciples	Hugh Thompson
Issues Facing Society	John Houghton
Living in the Anointing	Paul Scanlon
Money Matters	Stephen Matthew
More Than Conquerors	Don Silber
Realities of the New Creation	Dale Barnes
Secure in God	Tony & Margaret Howson
Successful Parents	Hugh & Rosemary Thompson
Woman: Created for Success	Barbie Reynolds
Woman: Living in Victory	Barbie Reynolds

Secure in God

Tony & Margaret Howson

Harvestime

Published in the United Kingdom by:
Harvestime Publishing Ltd, 69 Main Street
Markfield, Leicester LE6 0UT

First published by Harvestime under the title
Living in God's Security
First printed April 1988
Reprinted January 1992

ISBN 1-872877-08-7

Typeset in the United Kingdom by:
ScribeTech Ltd, Bradford BD8 7BX

Printed and bound in the United Kingdom by:
BPCC Hazell Books, Aylesbury, Bucks, England
Member of BPCC Ltd

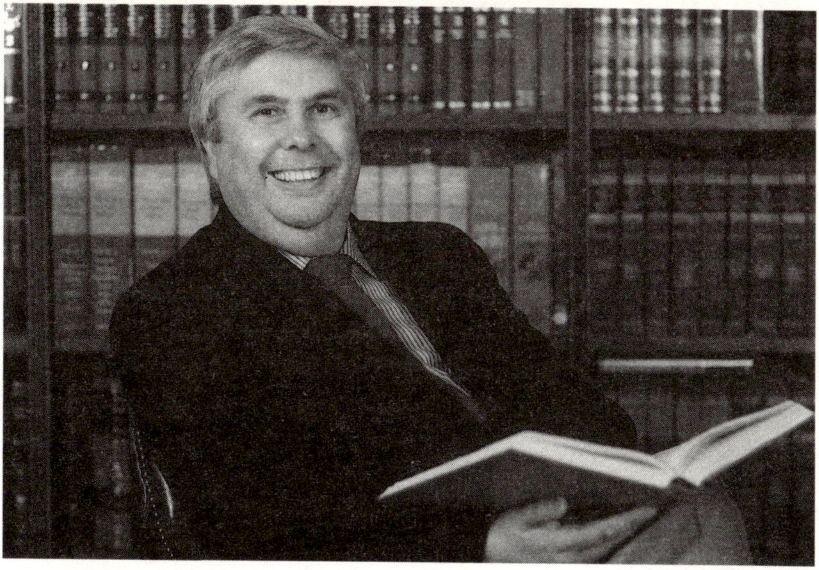

Increasing numbers of people are wanting to study the Word of God in depth. To go to a Bible college or seminary is not feasible for the majority, yet they desire more than the average church is able to provide in its teaching curriculum.

The book you are about to study is part of a library of components that together provide a comprehensive overview of the Scriptures in relation to life. Each book is complete in itself but is developed in such a way that the best result is experienced by studying it as part of the whole series.

We have produced the curriculum so that each component, in addition to its use as a personal study, can provide a seven-week teaching programme for study in church, home, college campus, school, military base, prison or any other group setting.

It is our prayer that you will be greatly enriched in your spiritual development through this book.

Bryn Jones
Founder — School of the Word

Getting the Most Out of This Study

This School of the Word study book is one of a series designed to relate Bible truths to everyday life. Each of the seven lessons starts with a direct search of the Scriptures and ends with a challenge to the student to apply the truths discovered. As the blank spaces left in Bible verses are filled in, the most important words and phrases stand out clearly on the page.

The material can be used in a number of different ways. It can form the basis of an individual study or be used in a group setting over a number of weeks. But experience has shown that it has the greatest benefit when a group of people study it together under a leader who is well prepared.

Tips for Leaders

If you are a leader planning to take a number of people through this study, you should consider the following:

1. Be prepared

It is essential that you do the whole study in advance yourself. This will help you to be conversant with the basic outline and have a feeling for the level of teaching based on it that your students can take.

2. Keep to the outline

It is important to keep to the outline contained in this study. This has been carefully designed to build principle on principle, 'precept upon precept' (Isaiah 28:10 RAV), with the eventual aim of the student becoming 'thoroughly equipped for every good work' (2 Timothy 3:17).

Whatever happens, don't allow your teaching to digress and become an opportunity to preach an hour's sermon!

3. Use your own experience

Even though you are staying with the outline, where possible introduce additional illustrations and applications drawn from your own experience. This makes the basic teaching more relevant to the local setting. In addition, you may wish to add more emphasis to certain points.

4. Avoid indigestion

Each lesson should take about an hour to complete. You may like to divide this into two half-hour sessions by arranging a short break for coffee and a chat halfway through. That way, the teaching is kept to manageable portions.

In some cases you may feel that the group discussion is of such vital importance to your local area that you want to spread each lesson over two weeks. If you do this, try to divide the questions at the end so that they are relevant to that week's teaching.

5. Have the right tools

Make sure that all the students have access to a copy of the New International Version of the Bible — upon which the book is based. Encourage them to fill in the blank spaces in advance but to leave answering the true/false questions until after each teaching session.

Tips for Students

Before you start the study you need to ask yourself: Am I really committed to growing as a disciple of Jesus Christ? If the answer is yes, then you're ready to proceed. Here are some immediate steps you can take to ensure maximum benefit from the course:

1. Determine your goal

This book is designed to help you achieve God's goal and destiny for you. It doesn't matter whether you are young or old, a recent convert or someone who has been a Christian for many years.

Today you are taking a step towards the fulfilment of your destiny.

Look ahead and see yourself as God desires you to be. Then confess your commitment: 'This is the kind of person I *will* become.'

2. Plan your progress

Your faith commitment to work through this book, and so take one more step towards becoming the person God intends you to be, must not only be pursued but measured in its progress. The apostle Paul said:

> *'By the grace given me I say to every one of you: Do not think of yourself more highly than you ought, but rather think of yourself with sober judgment, in accordance with the measure of faith God has given you.'*
>
> (Romans 12:3)

You know the kind of person you already are. You know the level of commitment you already have in your life. Now from this point determine how much time per day or week you are prepared to give to the study of the Word of God to achieve your goal.

At the end of each lesson in this study-book there is an opportunity for you to complete assignments and answer some Bible-based questions. This helps to fix the Word of God more firmly in your heart, and thus provide a reservoir of truth that the Holy Spirit can draw upon in the training of your life.

3. Recruit to the study course

Fellowship is one of the keys to Christian growth. The word 'fellowship' comes from the Greek word *koinonia*, which means to 'share things in common'.

Nothing will facilitate your progress as much as encouraging others to share in the same study programme with you, either on a personal basis or in a group. Share with each other the things you are learning and discovering in the Word of God and in life.

In this way you will be able to practise together much of what you study, and so strengthen each other in faith, just as 'iron sharpens iron' (Proverbs 27:17).

4. Set and maintain your standards

If this study is to be of maximum benefit to you, it must not be hurried. It is no use merely reading the written material and rushing the assignment. The book is designed to provoke you to your own searching and thinking, and to a demonstration of faith in God.

5. Check your progress

Once you have worked right through the book, ask your pastor or church leader to read through your answers. If he is satisfied that you have done your best to complete the questions, get him to send us a note to this effect. We will then forward a certificate for him to sign and present to you.

Your pastor is also the best person to monitor your progress and share your zeal to develop as a Christian disciple. If you are at college, university or in the armed forces, or for some other reason have no immediate access to a pastor, send us your book enclosing return postage and we will send it back to you with your certificate.

School of the Word
Harvestime Publishing Ltd
69 Main Street
Markfield
Leicester LE6 0UT
UK

Contents

Unless otherwise stated, Scripture quotations are taken from the New International Version.

Other versions referred to in this series include the New American Standard Bible (NASB), the Revised Authorised Version (RAV) and the Amplified Bible (Amp).

Verses have blank spaces for you to insert the missing words as you follow the Scriptures. This will deepen the impact of the Bible in your life.

Secure in Our Unchanging God

1. The Great 'I AM'

Who is God? A human being trying to describe God is rather like a motor-car trying to describe its designer – it is virtually impossible! Fortunately, the Bible is able to help us.

At the burning bush, when Moses asked who was sending him to deliver the people of Israel, God's reply was:

> *'I AM WHO I AM. This is what you are to say to the Israelites: "I AM has sent me to you."'*
>
> (Exodus 3:14)

Before the beginning of time God was around. He has always existed at every moment of time, in every circumstance, in every place. 'I AM' was not just an aspect of God which Moses needed to acknowledge; it was an unchanging truth to be recognised by everyone for ever:

> *'This is ____ ________ for ever, the name by which I am to be ________________ from generation to generation.'*
>
> (Exodus 3:15)

God is eternal. As he was with Moses, therefore, so he is with you now, wherever you may be, as you read these pages. Your ultimate security lies in that fact.

2. His Unchanging Nature

'I AM' means that God never changes. He isn't fickle. His character is unchanging and his decisions and actions are always in line with his character:

> *'I the Lord do not change.'*
>
> (Malachi 3:6)

We need to adjust our viewpoint and see God as he really is instead of looking at him from a limited human perspective. If we fail to do this, we will never be sure of God's immutable intentions towards us and towards the rest of humankind.

Because God is unchanging, so is his Word. What he caused to be written in the Bible remains true for ever; his eternal nature and unchanging character guarantee this for us. We have:

> *'A faith and knowledge resting on the hope of eternal life which God, who does not lie, promised before the beginning of time'.*
>
> (Titus 1:2)

The foundation of our security, then, is more than just the *existence* of God: it is also the fact that God *remains the same*. We all know unreliable people who break their promises or fail to finish a job. But God is never guilty on either score:

> *'God is not a man, that he should lie, nor a son of man, that he should change his mind. Does he __________ and then not ______? Does he _____________ and not _____________? I have received a command to bless; he has blessed, and __ _____________ ___________ ____.'*
>
> (Numbers 23:19-20)

This means that no-one can prevent God from being everything you need. Because he is for ever the same, he is a secure, stable foundation for your life.

3. His Character

Having established that God is unchanging, let us look at just a few of his attributes, knowing that they, too, are unchanging. He is:

a. Loving

God is more than a loving God; he actually *is* love (1 John 4:8). Human love can be unstable, but God's love remains constant towards all people (John 3:16). We can depend utterly on that fact:

> *'We know and rely on the love God has for us. God is love. Whoever lives in love lives in God, and God in him.'*
>
> (1 John 4:16)

The psalmist was so convinced about God's love continuing for ever that half of one of his psalms consists of the phrase, 'His love endures for ever' (Psalm 136).

b. Compassionate (merciful)

God is 'the Judge of all the earth' (Genesis 18:25), but his judgments are always in line with his compassion:

> *'Because of the Lord's great love we are not consumed, for ________ ________________________ ____________ ________. They are new every morning; great is your faithfulness.'*
>
> (Lamentations 3:22-23)

c. Holy

Many of today's influences are positively harmful. There are pressures to follow the crowd, just as the Israelites wanted to be like other nations and so asked for a king (see 1 Samuel 8). But it is comforting to know that God will never be swayed by unrighteous pressures, because he is *holy* (Isaiah 6:3).

Holiness means 'separation'. God's holiness means that he consciously separates himself from evil. He is light, and in him there is no darkness at all (1 John 1:5). We can be secure in the fact that God will never compromise either himself or us. In fact, he is *incapable* of doing so.

> *'Holy, holy, holy is the Lord God Almighty, who was, and is, and is to come.'*
>
> (Revelation 4:8)

d. Glorious

Many of God's attributes are a part of the manifestation of his *glory*.

When Moses asked to see his glory,

> *'The Lord came down in the cloud and stood there with him and proclaimed his name, the Lord.'*
>
> (Exodus 34:5)

Then, while he was manifesting his glory, God proclaimed his own eternal attributes:

> *'The Lord, the Lord, the ______________________ and ________________ God, slow to anger, abounding in ______ and ____________________, maintaining love to thousands, and ______________ wickedness, rebellion and sin'.*
>
> (Exodus 34:6-7)

4. His Faithfulness

God has always operated in faith. Everything he has initiated and created reminds us of that fact. In particular, he trusts people and gives them great liberty within his expectations. He gave freedom to Adam and Eve in Eden:

> *'You are free to eat from any tree in the garden; but you must not eat from the tree of the knowledge of good and evil, for when you eat of it you will surely die.'*
>
> (Genesis 2:16-17)

Among all the plant life in the garden, only one tree was not part of the freedom they could enjoy. In entrusting them with the care and cultivation of the garden, God was operating in faith towards them.

Earlier, God's entire act of creation had been in the realm of faith. He had not had to toil and struggle:

> *'He spoke, and it came to be; he commanded, and it stood firm.'*
>
> (Psalm 33:9)

God is able to do such mighty acts from a position of rest. He is never insecure about whether his word will come to pass, because he knows who he is and the authority he commands.

Faithfulness is rooted in *faith*; we cannot be faithful unless we have faith. Since God is not changeable, he is always operating in faith and in the faithfulness of his character:

> *'The Lord is ____________ to all his ____________ and loving towards all he has made.'*
>
> (Psalm 145:13)

5. His Word

God's Word, the Bible, is far more than a collection of disconnected statements. It is able to communicate life, liberty and clarity:

> *'The word of God is __________ and ____________. Sharper than any double-edged sword, it penetrates even to dividing soul and spirit, joints and marrow; it judges the thoughts and attitudes of the heart.'*
>
> (Hebrews 4:12)

God has spoken so that his people need not be doubtful or insecure. Through his Word we can know exactly what he is able to do for us. What God says therefore carries purpose for us, though its value depends on our *response* to what he is saying. Do you respond to Scripture and order your life by its guidelines?

Both the written Word of God and the spoken, prophetic word in particular situations are vital. We must not emphasise one to the exclusion of the other. The word of revelation will not contradict the written Word; on the contrary, it will always be in line with it, because:

> *'The word of our God stands for ever.'*
>
> (Isaiah 40:8)

People were astonished by the revolutionary words of Jesus, and the religious leaders even accused him of breaking God's written laws. But nothing Jesus said contradicted what God had spoken hundreds of years before. Jesus said:

> *'Do not think that I have come to abolish the Law or the Prophets; I have not come to abolish them but to fulfil them.'*
>
> (Matthew 5:17)

Since God's word has always been reliable and influential – from the point of creation, through the centuries and up to the present day – and will continue to be so in the future, we can be secure in everything God has said and is still saying. His word never changes, and there is no situation into which he cannot speak.

We must therefore see God's written Word, not as a negative list of rules and regulations, but as a reliable source of help, wisdom and direction in which we can find security.

6. His Interest in People

God has always shown an interest in humankind. He has never ceased loving each of us. Even when Adam and Eve had disgraced themselves by sinning, God still showed his fatherly and practical love for them:

> *'The Lord God made garments of skin for Adam and his wife and ______________ ________.'*
>
> (Genesis 3:21)

While it is possible for each of us to anger God, even in his anger he loves us and desires the best for us. There is no-one whom God does not love and towards whom he does not have compassion. Even previously wicked men and women have found God's protection when they have repented and cried out to him for help:

> *'The Lord is righteous in all his ways and loving towards all he has made. The Lord is near to all who call on him, to all who call on him in truth. He fulfils the desires of those who fear him; he hears their cry and saves them.'*
>
> (Psalm 145:17-19)

God's concern for us isn't influenced by what we have been, said or done. True to himself, he deals with us according to his love and compassion (see Psalm 103:1-12).

7. His Desire to Guide

In that love of his, God watches over us and protects us:

> *'O Lord, you have ______________ me and you ________ me. You know when I sit and when I rise; you _______________ my ______________ from afar. You discern my going out and my lying down; you are familiar with ______ ____ ________.'*
>
> (Psalm 139:1-3)

But God's interest is not only for the present; he wants to guide us into the future so that we achieve worthwhile goals and experience fulfilment under his loving direction. He will guide us through his written Word (Psalm 119:105), but he also wants to speak with us specifically so that we achieve those goals by the best possible means:

> *'You guide me with your counsel, and afterwards you will take me into glory . . . . My flesh and my heart may fail, but God is the strength of my heart and my portion for ever.'*
>
> (Psalm 73:24, 26)

He will speak to our heart as we seek him in prayer. He will also guide us by prophecy, wise counsel and our circumstances.

8. Everything for Our Best

Only God is able to lead us into the best for our lives because he alone understands all that is happening. He is aware not only of our past and present but also of the future – and can therefore discern situations better than we can.

Sometimes, to our natural understanding, our own way of doing things may appear easier and more direct than God's. But God's ways are always best:

> *'A man's steps are directed by the Lord. How then can anyone understand his own way?'*
>
> (Proverbs 20:24)

So God knows what is best for us. He also understands how we can achieve it. As we place our confidence in him, he gives us the desires of our hearts (Psalm 37:4). And as we become more secure in him we find growing confidence in his choice of the best way forward:

> *'Commit to the Lord ________________ ______ ____ ,*
> *and your ________ will ____________ .'*
>
> (Proverbs 16:3)

Remember, God isn't clinically plotting a graph for our existence. He loves us, and this love is his motivation in working things for our good:

> *'We know that in ______ __________ God works for the ________ of those who love him, who have been called according to his purpose.'*
>
> (Romans 8:28)

'*All* things' includes things we don't like – setbacks, disappointments, hurts, etc. Paul battled against satanic powers, but by faith he knew that God would cause those difficulties to work for his good. How frustrating for Satan to see that, in the end, his efforts work out for the good of God's children! Who, then, is more insecure than Satan, and who more secure than us?

LESSON 1

Secure in Our Unchanging God

True or False

1. T F God never changes.
2. T F God's love for a person endures for as long as that person loves him in return.
3. T F The entire act of creation was accomplished from a position of rest because God knows who he is and what authority he commands.
4. T F God is only faithful to those who are faithful to him.
5. T F The Bible – God's Word – still speaks to people today.
6. T F After Adam and Eve sinned, God lost interest in them.
7. T F God wants to guide my life, helping me to achieve worthwhile goals.
8. T F God's ways are always the best.
9. T F God seeks only my highest good.

Group Discussion

1. God said, 'I AM WHO I AM.' What does this mean? How does it help us to understand who God is?

2. How can we be secure in a God we cannot see?

Personal Assignment

1. Compile a list of the attributes of God so that you can learn what he is like. You might also like to read a book on the subject, such as A.W. Tozer's *The Knowledge of the Holy*.

2. Decide to begin thinking of God in *bigger* terms.

True or False

1.T 2.F 3.T 4.F 5.T 6.F 7.T 8.T 9.T

Christ – Our Sure Foundation

Through his life and ministry Jesus brought more than teaching. He brought to us the ways of the Lord, a path on which we could tread securely. In doing this, *Jesus himself* became the foundation upon whom we can build a secure relationship with God the Father (1 Corinthians 3:11).

Let us therefore examine certain aspects of Jesus' ministry on our behalf.

1. The Cross

From almost the beginning of time, the problem which prevented men and women from having a free, open and loving relationship with God was their own sins. Throughout Bible history, people offered sacrifices to God to atone for their sin.

At Calvary, Jesus became a sin-offering (2 Corinthians 5:21), sacrificing himself to appease the holiness of God, for the benefit of those who put their faith in his death. Peace with God, previously unavailable to humankind, suddenly became a real possibility – however sinful their past life had been. God's purpose was:

'Through him to ________________ to himself all things, whether things on earth or things in heaven, by making __________ through his blood, shed on the cross'.

(Colossians 1:20)

The sacrifice of Jesus was sufficient for all people and for all time.

2. The Resurrection

At the cross Jesus took our sins. In rising again from death he gave us the authority to act on earth as the true people of God. Where there had once been death, there could now be life for every believer:

'He was delivered over to death for our sins and was raised to life for our justification.'

(Romans 4:25)

In rising from the dead, Jesus proved the validity of his earlier statements. When he stated, for example, that he had authority not only to lay down his life but also to take it up again (John 10:18), the claim had not been proved. By his resurrection the truth of his claim was fully ratified. This means that we can be *confident* about the statements and claims he made.

3. The Ascension

It is part of a secure home situation for a child to know that he has his parents' approval in what he does. Within the youngster there is a deep-seated feeling of satisfaction, fulfilment and total acceptability when a loving parent rewards his or her obedience.

The ascension of Jesus into heaven and his taking again of his rightful place at the right hand of his Father (Mark 16:19) proved that Jesus was accepted not only as a Son and heir but also as one who had done all things well and obtained his Father's complete approval. God himself is satisfied by the ministry of Jesus, and that includes his ministry on our behalf – a comforting truth!

Jesus, having received the approval of his Father, was able to be seated. He could be at ease knowing that he had totally fulfilled his commission. We, too, can be secure in knowing that Jesus acted not only for his own satisfaction but also for the pleasure of his Father – and for our eternal benefit.

4. The Holy Spirit

a. Sent

Not until Jesus had ascended into heaven was he able to send the promised Holy Spirit (John 7:39). The Holy Spirit was sent to the disciples from Jesus' exalted position:

> *'I am going to send you what my Father has promised; but stay in the city until you have been clothed with power from on high.'*
>
> (Luke 24:49)

The Holy Spirit's coming (Acts 2:1-4) attested, first, to the ascension of Jesus and, second, to God's approval of Jesus' followers on earth:

> *'You . . . were included in Christ when you heard the word of truth, the gospel of ______ ______________. Having believed, you were marked in him with a seal, the promised Holy Spirit, who is a deposit ____________________ our inheritance until the redemption of those who are God's possession – to the praise of his glory.'*
>
> (Ephesians 1:13-14)

When we pay a deposit on, say, a house or car, we are indicating our full intention to complete the purchase. In a similar way, we can be secure in the fact that those to whom God has given the deposit of his Holy Spirit will not be deserted by him. Having paid the deposit, he is determined to continue the good work he has begun in us until it is complete when Jesus Christ returns (Philippians 1:6).

b. Received

God sent his Holy Spirit as a gift and, like every gift, the Holy Spirit needs to be *received*. God our Father wants to give us good gifts. As we become secure in his fatherhood, we can be confident in receiving the gift of the Holy Spirit because God will not withhold him from us:

> *'If you . . . though you are evil, know how to give good gifts to your children, how much more will your Father in heaven give the Holy Spirit to those who ask him!'*
>
> (Luke 11:13)

We can be confident in asking, knowing that we *will* receive. Expect to receive the Holy Spirit – you will know about it when you do!

c. For all generations

Before Pentecost the Holy Spirit had been much in evidence in the Old Testament and throughout the ministry of Jesus. But at Pentecost came the lasting anointing which Jesus had foretold:

> *'I will ask the Father, and he will give you another Counsellor to be________ ______ ______ ________ – the Spirit of truth. The world cannot accept him, because it neither sees him nor knows him. But you know him, for he lives with you and will be ____ ______.'*
>
> (John 14:16-17)

God wants all believers to have the gift of the Holy Spirit, no matter where they come from, what they may have done or in which generation they may be living. Peter, preaching to the crowds at Jerusalem, affirmed this when he said:

> *'You will receive the gift of the Holy Spirit. The promise is ______ ______ and ________ ________________ and for all who are far off – for______ whom the Lord our God will call.'*
>
> (Acts 2:38-39)

5. Liberty

When travelling salesmen try to sell 'security systems' they are talking about objects or buildings being locked up so that no-one can get in, affording maximum protection. 'Maximum security' prisons exist to make it as difficult as possible for internees to escape their imprisonment.

Security in God is not like that. In coming to Jesus, we find that, far from being 'locked up', we are set free so that we are able to live life to the full (John 10:10). The security God wants us to enjoy is more like that of children whose father desires their best, loves them to the uttermost and works all things for their good so that they can grow into fulfilled maturity:

> *'It is for freedom that Christ has set us free.'*
>
> (Galatians 5:1)

Instead of being bound by oppressive rules and regulations, life in God becomes fulfilling, satisfying, adventurous and purposeful. Under the Lord's shepherding care we enjoy variety in life, coming in and going out and finding pasture (John 10:9). In every sense, salvation and becoming secure in God bring true release.

6. Springboard

It is exciting to see a swimmer leap from a springboard and make a successful dive into water, or to see a gymnast perform a difficult vault by leaping from a springboard. In both cases, for a few seconds the person is apparently liberated from the law of gravity and sails through the air.

Security in God can become a springboard into fulness of life and activity. The Bible calls it 'life in the Spirit' – a quality of life beyond that of everyday, mundane existence. God wants his people happy, and he has provided everything we need to make it possible.

> *'Whoever drinks the water I give him will never thirst. Indeed, the water I give him will become in him a spring of water welling up to eternal life.'*
>
> (John 4:14)

God wants the 'spring of water' within us – the life of the Spirit – to continue to well up. He does not give us an experience of the Holy Spirit for it to become a spiritual 'historic monument'. While it is true that our whole life in him comes out of a past experience, we must move forward in continuing faith and expectation.

A trainee gymnast uses a springboard to execute basic vaults over a piece of apparatus. As he becomes more experienced and proficient he uses the same springboard to execute more difficult vaults. Once we are secure in our experience of God we can move on to greater achievements, growing in confidence and finding increasing joy.

7. Destiny

God did not save us just because he thought it was a good idea! The Bible makes it clear that he called us 'according to his purpose' (Romans 8:28). God has plans! It is no surprise, therefore, to find that he projects hopes, aspirations and ambitions into each of us. He wants us to be successful, to achieve something.

As we understand this, there grows within us an enthusiasm to do the works that God wants us to do. It is an enthusiasm born of our God-given 'joy in the Holy Spirit' (Romans 14:17), making us an enthusiastic people, zealous to achieve for him.

A child learning to ride a bicycle at first struggles to keep his balance, mainly because he is insecure and frightened to go too quickly. If he pedalled faster he would find he could balance much better. So it is with the people of God. The more involved we get with God's purpose and goals, the less concerned we become for things of the past and the more confident we are in reaching forward:

> *'I press on to take hold of that for which Christ Jesus took hold of me . . . . One thing I do: Forgetting what is behind and straining towards what is ahead, I press on towards the goal to win the prize for which God has called me heavenwards in Christ Jesus.'*
>
> (Philippians 3:12-14)

Having received the Holy Spirit, we may be confident that God isn't just leaving us to our own devices. The Spirit is working with us, so that we may know success:

> *'Always give yourselves fully to the work of the Lord, because you know that your labour in the Lord is ______ ____ ________.'*
>
> (1 Corinthians 15:58)

Our confident looking towards God will provide us with a foundation of security upon which we can build with freedom of expression to see God's purposes fulfilled.

> *'Being __________ of this, that he who ______ a good work in you will carry it on to ________________ until the day of Christ Jesus'.*
>
> (Philippians 1:6)

****

LESSON 2

Christ – Our Sure Foundation

True or False

1. T F In order to maintain an ongoing relationship with God we must continually make sacrifices to atone for our sin.

2. T F The literal resurrection of Jesus means that we can be confident about the statements and claims he made.

3. T F The Father is satisfied by the ministry of Jesus, including his ministry on our behalf.

4. T F The Holy Spirit is forced upon everyone, regardless of whether or not they want to receive him.

5. T F The Holy Spirit ceased to operate after New Testament times.

6. T F Life in Jesus is bound by lots of rules which make it very boring.
7. T F Life in Jesus gives us freedom so that we are able to live life to the full.
8. T F God wants us to be secure in our experience of him so that we can be successful in life.
9. T F The more involved we get in God's purpose and goal, the less concerned we become for things of the past and the more confident we are in reaching forward.

Group Discussion

1. How do Christ's resurrection and ascension, as well as his cross, affect our daily Christian living?
2. How do non-Christians try to find security? How does that compare with security in God?
3. Why is it necessary to have a firm foundation to launch out in God? Give some practical illustrations.

Personal Assignment

1. Find scriptures to show the presence of the Holy Spirit in Old Testament times, New Testament times and the present day.
2. Think of at least six times when you have been aware of God's Spirit leading you. If you have difficulty finding six, ask God to speak to you clearly, then make yourself

available to respond to his leading more promptly and regularly, till it becomes a way of life.

True or False

1.F 2.T 3.T 4.F 5.F 6.F 7.T 8.T 9.T

Secure in Our Inheritance

So far, we have looked at who God is, and we have seen something of his nature and character as expressed in Jesus. Now we will look at some of the great privileges we have inherited as his children – all calculated to strengthen our sense of security in him.

1. God's Perspective

To become increasingly secure in our relationship with God, we need to begin looking at ourselves from his viewpoint. His mind can then renew our minds, and his security will be ours. What does the Bible have to say about us?

In Christ:

☐ We are not downtrodden (Proverbs 28:1)

☐ We are not weak (Ephesians 6:10)

☐ We are not insignificant (Matthew 10:29-31)

On the contrary, in him:

☐ We are triumphant (2 Corinthians 2:14)

☐ We are victorious (Philippians 4:13)

☐ We are confident (2 Corinthians 3:4)

Look for other Bible references for each of these categories. It is our privilege to reign like kings in the circumstances of life:

> *'If, by the trespass of the one man, death reigned through that one man, how much more will those who ______________ God's abundant provision of grace and of the ________ of righteousness ___________ ____ ________ through the one man, Jesus Christ.'*
>
> (Romans 5:17)

2. Chosen

a. We are hand-picked!

Yes, it is really true! In spite of all our faults, problems and hang-ups, God actually chose each of us individually to be part of his kingdom:

> *'He __________ ____ in him before the creation of the world to be holy and blameless in his sight.'*
>
> (Ephesians 1:4)

We don't have to justify our inclusion in the kingdom of God. We simply have to accept it. Enter your name in the blank space at the end of the following statement:

Before the world was created God chose ____________________ _______________________ .

b. It is a gift – by grace

It is impossible to *earn* a place in the kingdom of God. We saw in the last lesson that the only basis for our inclusion in the kingdom of God is our salvation in Christ.

We are accepted because Jesus has secured a place for us. There is nothing more to be done. We cannot add to a work which is complete:

> *'God . . . has saved us and called us to a holy life – not because of anything we have done but because of his own purpose and grace.'*
>
> (2 Timothy 1:8-9)

c. It is God's choice, not ours

God has chosen many people, all of whom he accepts on the same conditions of entry – repentance and faith in Jesus. If they are accepted by God we, too, must accept them. God shows no partiality – and neither should we.

> *'As God's chosen people, holy and dearly loved, clothe yourselves with compassion, kindness, humility, gentleness and patience. Bear with each other and forgive whatever grievances you may have against one another. Forgive as the Lord forgave you.'*
>
> (Colossians 3:12-13)

For some people, the difficulty is not in accepting the fact that others are chosen, but in accepting the fact of their own inclusion. The truth remains: God chose each one and each is precious in his sight. What a source of security!

3. A Child of God

Regardless of our earthly parents (Romans 9:8), when we are born again we become children of God (1 John 3:1). We are born anew into his family and he becomes our Father:

> *'To all who received him, to those who ____________ in his name, he gave the right to become __________________ ____ ______ – children born not of natural descent, nor of human decision or a husband's will, but born of God.'*
>
> (John 1:12-13)

God accepts us as sons and daughters and commits himself to being a heavenly Father to us. How do we respond? Are we committed to living obediently as children of God, or are we still saying in our hearts, 'I'll do it my way'?

As a Father, God provides for his children. We can be secure in the knowledge that God not only knows our needs but will also meet them:

> *'My God will meet ________ __________ __________ according to his glorious riches in Christ Jesus.'*
>
> (Philippians 4:19)

We should not expect God to meet our needs according to our own limited thinking, but from the *wealth of his riches* (Psalm 50:9-12). God will meet the need abundantly! He loves a cheerful giver *and* a cheerful receiver. Are we ready and willing to receive all he has for us?

4. Heirs

Children inherit from their family. Their inheritance – great or small – may be bestowed on them either during the lifetime or at the death of their parents. Money, gifts, titles, estate, material items – an inheritance can come in many forms; or it might not come at all.

But there is no 'might' or 'maybe' about our inheritance as God's children. We are all entitled to an inheritance in his heavenly kingdom:

> *'The Spirit himself testifies with our spirit that we are God's children. Now if we are children, then we are heirs – heirs of God and co-heirs with Christ.'*
>
> (Romans 8:16-17)

As children of God, we have a right to claim our inheritance. Much of what God has for us is available to us *now* in Christ – we don't have to wait.

Like an inheritance from natural parents, our *super*natural inheritance comes in many forms. God has bestowed on us 'every spiritual blessing' (Ephesians 1:3): family, homes and land (Mark 10:30); eternal life (Titus 3:7); and many good and perfect gifts (James 1:17).

5. Seated in Heavenly Places

Jesus is seated at God's right hand in the heavenly realms (Ephesians 1:20). Spiritually speaking, we are there with him:

> *'God raised us up with Christ and ____________ ____ with him in the ________________ ____________ in Christ Jesus.'*
>
> (Ephesians 2:6)

If we are seated with Christ in heavenly places, we can look down on our problems. From down below, the problems and difficulties can look enormous. But from above, looking down, they seem minute, almost too small to see. We know they are still there, but they don't tower over us and dominate our lives. We can see the situation from God's viewpoint.

Are we seated there in practice? Or are we still rushing around trying to sort things out ourselves? It is our privilege to rest secure in the completed work of Jesus and reign with him:

> *'Do not be anxious about anything, but in everything, by prayer and petition, with thanksgiving, present your requests to God.'*
>
> (Philippians 4:6)

6. Free from Condemnation

We often say, 'It'll turn out all right in the end.' Many Christians live with the view that *one day* we shall be holy and free from condemnation.

But that day is *now!*

> *'There is ______ no condemnation for those who are in Christ Jesus.'*
>
> (Romans 8:1)

It will all turn out right in the end, too, of course. Our likeness to Jesus will then be complete (1 John 3:2). But why leave everything until the end of our lives? Live free from condemnation now! Every type of condemnation undermines your security.

Avoid negative confessions:

'Failed again'

'I'll never make it'

'I can't'

'I'm not perfect' (None of us are, but we are aiming for maturity in Christ. See Colossians 1:28.)

Instead, confess the Word of God:

> *'I can do everything through him who gives me strength.'*
>
> (Philippians 4:13)

> *'Everyone born of God overcomes the world.'*
>
> (1 John 5:4)

> *'He gives strength to the weary and increases the power of the weak.'*
>
> (Isaiah 40:29)

7. Powerful Through Discipline

a. A well-equipped army

God never intended the church to be timid and hesitant. He has made complete provision for us as his army, to be equipped and protected in every way. We need to wear the whole armour of God (see Ephesians 6:10-18) in order to fight the good fight of faith (1 Timothy 6:12).

A well-trained army doesn't give the impression of being timid or easily intimidated. Its soldiers are well-disciplined, powerful and effective.

> *'The word of God is living and active. Sharper than any double-edged sword . . . .'*
>
> (Hebrews 4:12)

Do we use this sword effectively?

> *'[He] is able to do immeasurably more than all we ask or imagine, according to ______ __________ that is at work ____________ _____ . . . .'*
>
> (Ephesians 3:20)

b. A disciplined people

Are we powerful, loving and self-disciplined? We should be, because:

> *'God did not give us a spirit of timidity, but a spirit of power, of love and of self-discipline.'*
>
> (2 Timothy 1:7)

We can learn much from a country's armed forces regarding discipline, particularly the lesson that, through it, unity is maintained and maximum effectiveness achieved.

It is important to differentiate between a *disciplined* life and a *religious* life. Scripture encourages the former (1 Timothy 4:7).

Disciplining our lives includes spending regular time in prayer and in God's Word, learning Scripture and applying it to our daily lives, so that it literally becomes the *living* word.

As we learn and quote the Word of God, it strengthens us and builds us up. We become secure in our knowledge of God – it is not merely a head-knowledge of facts but a living heart-knowledge of a living God.

Discipline isn't just something we exercise; it is also something we *receive* as sons and daughters of our heavenly Father. He disciplines us, as he did Jesus, through the often hard experiences of life:

> *'Although he was a son, he learned obedience from what he suffered.'*
>
> (Hebrews 5:8)

We need not fear God's discipline. It is born out of a heart of love. God's loving discipline keeps us free from condemnation and secure in the lordship of Jesus.

> *'When we are judged by the Lord, we are being ______________________ so that we will _______ _____ _________________ with the world.'*
>
> (1 Corinthians 11:32)

For any power to be effective it must first be harnessed. The mighty power of the mountain river is harnessed by the dam and its turbines to produce electricity. The power in our lives is God's Spirit; it needs harnessing by the loving discipline of our heavenly Father to cause us to become a united and effective people. True discipline will make us effective disciples.

****

LESSON 3

Secure in Our Inheritance

True or False

1. T F In spite of my faults, problems and hang-ups, God chose me to be part of his kingdom.
2. T F For some people, it might be difficult accepting the fact that others are chosen by God, but it is never a problem to accept the fact of their *own* inclusion.
3. T F Because I am his child, God wants to meet my needs abundantly.
4. T F I can claim my inheritance of eternal life only when I die.
5. T F I am seated with Christ in heavenly places and can rest secure in his completed work.
6. T F I can live free from condemnation *now!*

7. T F Because God loves us he will not discipline us if it hurts us.

8. T F God's loving discipline keeps us free from condemnation.

Group Discussion

1. What factors can cause a Christian not to believe in or accept his security in Christ?

2. What advice can we offer to such insecure believers?

3. What can we learn about family life from the way God disciplines us as his children? See Hebrews 12:4-13.

Personal Assignment

1. Find in the New Testament three things not discussed in this lesson that the Bible says we are in Christ. Apply them to your own life.

2. Focus on two areas mentioned in the lesson where you know there is room for improvement in your own life. Think and pray about how you can improve in these areas, then share your thoughts and decisions with a close Christian friend.

True or False

1.T 2.F 3.T 4.F 5.T 6.T 7.F 8.T

Secure in the Church

1. What is the Church?

People have strange ideas about what the church really is. Some would see it as a denominational organisation holding Sunday services. Others, with buildings and 'holy' places foremost in their thinking, would say it is a stone structure with a spire and stained-glass windows.

In fact, the church is *people*. Whenever the Bible refers to church, it always means God's redeemed people, those who have received salvation through the merits of Jesus. People who have not come into a true relationship with God would not be counted by him as part of his church, even though they may belong to a religious organisation.

The New Testament church was foretold in the Old Testament:

> *'They will be called the Holy People, the Redeemed of the Lord; and you will be called* ***Sought After****, the City No Longer Deserted.'*
>
> (Isaiah 62:12)

'Sought After' – God is always seeking a people through whom he can fulfil his purpose of declaring his glory throughout the earth. One day,

'The earth will be __________ with the __________ of the __________ ____ ______ ________, as the waters cover the sea.'

(Habakkuk 2:14)

This will happen as the church increases numerically and as each individual Christian is changed from one degree of glory to another (2 Corinthians 3:18).

2. An Optional Extra?

Some Christians ask, 'Do I *have* to be involved in the church?'

The answer is 'yes'. It was never God's intention that Christians should be independent and individualistic. He frequently refers to 'my people' collectively. Though at one time we were outside the church, salvation has brought us into the church, thus making us a part of the people of God:

'Once you were not a people, but now you are the __________ ____ ______; once you had not received mercy, but now you have __________ __________.'

(1 Peter 2:10)

Each individual is involved as a part of the whole. The church is the 'body of Christ':

'You are the body of Christ, and each one of you is a part of it.'

(1 Corinthians 12:27)

If part of the body isn't functioning correctly, the whole body is affected. Therefore, God expects us *all* to be involved:

> *'The body is a unit, though it is made up of ________ __________; and though all its parts are many, they form ______ ________.'*
>
> (1 Corinthians 12:12)

3. Fellowship

It is easy for fear to strike at us when we contemplate the idea of being involved with the people of God. Questions like 'Will they accept me?' and 'Am I too unimportant?' can colour our thinking. But God has received each of us on exactly the same basis and, as part of the body, you can help others. They actually need your help! In what ways?

a. Spiritual contribution

New Christians may well feel unable to do some of the things they see more mature Christians doing, such as preaching or leading worship. But even the newest Christian has *some* part to play. God wants us to know that we have a contribution to make for the spiritual good of everyone:

> *'When you come together,* ***everyone*** *has a hymn, or a word of instruction, a revelation, a tongue or an interpretation. All of these must be done for the strengthening of the church.'*
>
> (1 Corinthians 14:26)

Even if you don't feel ready to do some of these things, or have not yet received prophetic revelation, remember that we can all pray, worship, recount God's goodness to us and encourage one another. And not just during meetings but also afterwards, perhaps complimenting brothers or sisters on their obedience to the Lord in speaking out what they received.

Since God wants to use each one of us, we must be secure in God's desire to use us in these areas and, like Paul, be prepared to venture forth in the realms of the Spirit (2 Corinthians 12:1).

b. Practical contribution

God has given people different gifts and skills. Not everyone is able to preach – but they may be gifted to serve the church in practical ways.

Cleaning and preparing the church premises for the meeting, mowing the lawn for the infirm, carrying heavy shopping for the elderly, helping one another with decorating a room – these are just a few expressions of practical service. And even if you don't consider yourself practically skilled in any area, you can at least occasionally babysit for parents who *are*, thus releasing them to do their part in the church.

If God has given us an ability, he wants us to use it in the context of the church. Not only does God want it, his people want it as well! False modesty about your abilities ('I'm not much good at it really') is a form of pride. Admit your gifts and use them. You will find security in knowing you have something of value to contribute to the life of the church.

4. You Count

You are important. You are important to God – that is why he saved you and put you in his church. It follows, therefore, that you must also be important to his people – probably far more than you realise.

At the moment, you may be suffering or going through a tough time, and feel you have nothing to give. Then be secure in receiving from your brothers and sisters in the church. Your hurts become God's hurts and, as you suffer, his people suffer with you:

> *'There should be no division in the body, but . . . its parts should have equal concern for each other. If ______ ________ suffers, __________ ________ suffers with it; if ______ ________ is honoured, __________ ________ rejoices with it.'*
>
> (1 Corinthians 12:25-26)

Soon, you will once again be in a position to bless your fellow-Christians. In the meantime you still count!

5. Your Attributes

Don't allow foolish comparisons to rob you of your security. Don't let another person's gift cause you to feel jealous or inadequate. God will honour those – including you – who are neither full of self-importance nor threatened by what others in his church can do.

'Those parts of the body that seem to be weaker are indispensable, and the parts that we think are less honourable we treat with special honour.'

(1 Corinthians 12:22-23)

God has intentionally not made us alike. Just as in the human body every limb, gland and organ has been positioned to perform a unique function, so too in the spiritual body – the church – each of us has his or her own function.

Consider, for example, how this study has reached you. To begin with, the authors had some ideas and jotted them down on paper, but much skilled work was needed to bring those ideas to their present completed form.

First, someone had to type up the manuscript. Then postal workers were involved in sending it to the editors, who revised and improved it before passing it on to the typesetters and then to the printers.

The printed pages were then cut and bound in the correct order. Someone packed copies together and sent them by post or delivery service either directly to you or to the bookshop where you purchased your copy. All these people – and more – were involved at various stages, according to their skills, to achieve the best result for you.

This is how you should see yourself in the church, as a unique and useful part of the whole. What you *can* do, and what you *enjoy* doing, is an asset to the church and to God's purpose for it. Be secure in that fact.

6. Your Belongings

The early disciples 'had everything in common' (Acts 2:44). They considered their homes and possessions to be for the benefit of God and his church, rather than their own exclusive property. Whether our property is a tent or a mansion, it is of greatest use when shared.

God expects us to retain responsibility for our own homes and possessions, but he doesn't want us to be grasping or selfish with them. Rather, he wants us to use them to express our love to one another. Hospitality and practical mutual care for one another are visual expressions of the love God has put in our hearts – and they are a powerful tool in evangelism:

> *'All men will know that you are my disciples, if you love one another.'*
>
> (John 13:35)

Where we can help one another with our belongings – lending our car, for example – we should feel free to do that. But when someone has lent something to us, we should respect that person by being a good steward and using their property in an honourable way.

If the tent we borrow is sent back with a broken zip, or the car has an extra dent in its bumper, the lender won't feel so ready to offer us the use of them another time.

Don't look for security in your belongings. Your security must be first in God and then in making your belongings available to him through his people – a way of 'losing your life' in order to gain it (see Matthew 10:39).

7. Church Responsibilities

When we agree, at the church leaders' request, to serve the church in some specific way, we must appreciate that with the responsibility comes authority.

If we accept responsibility for stacking chairs at the end of the meeting, for example, we should feel free to ask people to help us, so that the job can be completed quickly and efficiently. We should not be silently resentful if we feel someone isn't co-operating with us; we must be able to lovingly encourage them to work alongside us to get the job done.

The principle works both ways, of course, and we must be willing to help and encourage others in their responsibilities, so that they, too, may be efficient and effective in what they do for God. There is great security in sharing each other's burdens this way.

As the word suggests, *respons*ibility involves response. God expects us to be responsive in everything – in worship, preaching and teaching, and, whenever there is a general appeal for help and we have the necessary ability, in being willing to share the workload. Special church ventures always require additional manpower. Our willingness to serve will encourage others and also help non-Christians to see love working in co-operation.

Are you secure in your church role? Then share the blessing – a pat on the back or word of encouragement will cause others to be even more secure in their responsibilities, too.

LESSON 4

Secure in the Church

True or False

1. T F The church consists of many buildings – for example, cathedrals, chapels, abbeys, monasteries.
2. T F Every Christian is part of the church, the 'body of Christ'.
3. T F If I am not fulfilling my role, the whole body suffers.
4. T F It is unlikely that a new believer will have any contribution to make for the spiritual good of others.
5. T F I can find security by knowing that I have something of value to contribute to the life of the church.
6. T F Even if I am going through a difficult time, I am important to God and also to his people.
7. T F Some people are useful to God while others have little or no part to play in the church.
8. T F My home cannot be used to bless others unless it is big and expensively furnished.
9. T F Security in the church comes when people are willing to share each other's burdens by helping one another in their specific responsibilities.

Group Discussion

1. Let each member of the group say briefly how he or she sees his or her contribution to the body of Christ.

2. Suggest ways in which you could make yourselves and your belongings more readily available to one another.

3. What differences would it make to the local body of Christ if you decided to leave?

Personal Assignment

1. Assess your part in the body of Christ. Are you fulfilled? Are there areas where you could be further involved?

2. What, apart from specific responsibilities, are you actively doing to help others be secure in the church?

True or False

1.F 2.T 3.T 4.F 5.T 6.T 7.F 8.F 9.T

Secure in Relationships

1. Personal Security

As we become more secure in God we become secure in our relationships with other people. Relationships involve more than head-knowledge; they are a matter of the heart. To know *about* God is not necessarily to *know* him. We may know a lot about Her Majesty the Queen, but most of us cannot claim to know her in any personal way. Let us see how this applies:

a. Our relationship with God

Open your heart to God, being confident that he knows and loves you. He not only cares about us now, but he cared about us from the moment of conception – he loved us even before our parents knew we existed!

> *'Before I formed you in the womb I knew you, before you were born I set you apart.'*
>
> (Jeremiah 1:5)

(See also Psalm 139:13-16.)

This means that God has been lovingly involved with us from the beginning of our life. We need have no shame or regrets about our legitimacy, shape, size or sex – God makes no mistakes and loves us the way we are. He created us either male or female, and what we are is what he intended us to be. The very fact that God wants to be recognised as our *Father* shows his involvement in all these matters.

God isn't ashamed of us, so we have no right to be ashamed of ourselves with regard to who we are. And if we are ashamed of what we've *done*, our heartfelt repentance will bring God's loving forgiveness (see 1 John 1:9).

Jesus, too, is happy to be associated with us:

> *'Both the one who makes men holy and those who are made holy are of the ________ ____________ . So Jesus is not ashamed to call them ________________ .'*
>
> (Hebrews 2:11)

b. Our relationship with others

Since the Lord has accepted us and is not ashamed of us, we need never be ashamed of ourselves or lacking in confidence in the presence of other people. They have no right to reject us when God has accepted us. But even if they do, we can remain secure in the Lord's acceptance.

2. Families

a. Our parents

We can easily become dissatisfied with our natural parents. But to God it doesn't matter who they are or what they may have done. His ability to shape our lives for his glory is not limited by our parents and other relatives. Our security in our relationship with God will enable us to maintain a loving and patient attitude towards even the most difficult of parents. We will honour them out of obedience to him (Exodus 20:12; Ephesians 6:1-3).

b. Our partner (or lack of one)

Whether we are married or single, we can be like the apostle Paul, who said:

> *'I have learned to be content whatever the circumstances.'*
>
> (Philippians 4:11)

Single people should not feel deprived or ashamed, as if singleness was some kind of problem. Jesus was single. So was Paul.

Married people should rest secure in the fact that God will help us make the best of our marriage, even if we think we married the wrong partner. That way, our relationship will not be undermined by emotional instability.

If you are married to an unbeliever, you must be secure in this as well and continue not just to *exist* in the relationship but to *work at it,* with God's help, to see it improve. If, despite your best efforts, your unbelieving partner wants to end the relationship, Scripture makes allowance for that (see 1 Corinthians 7:12-16).

God doesn't hold the mistakes of the past against any of us, provided we have repented. It does no good to keep reminding ourselves of mistakes we have made. Instead, let us determine to learn from them and put them behind us, just as God has done.

c. Our children

Children are a blessing from the Lord, intended to make us glad (Proverbs 15:20; Psalm 127:3). Are our children secure in their relationship with us?

How we talk to them is important. We are to be firm yet loving and patient with them, not exasperating them (Ephesians 6:4) but bringing them up in a manner befitting God's people:

> '__________ __ __________ *in the way he should go, and when he is old he will* ______ ________ ________ ____.'
>
> (Proverbs 22:6)

Be secure in your ability, under God, to be a successful father or mother. Husband and wife should support one another in disciplining their children, resisting the temptation to contradict each other. A united front makes for secure children as well as contented parents.

Children, for their part, should not be ashamed of acknowledging their parents in front of their friends:

> *'Children's children are a crown to the aged, and parents are the pride of their children.'*
>
> (Proverbs 17:6)

Single people, in co-operation with parents, can have a useful role in children's lives. If you are single, consider how you can get alongside one or more children in the church, befriending them, taking them out on trips or teaching them practical skills.

3. Other People

Jealousy is a great divider. Contentment with our own situation will enable us not to be threatened by others or the things they possess or can do. It is a measure of your personal security that you can be grateful to God for the ways in which he has blessed them.

Whether married, single, retired or still living with our parents, we should always feel secure enough to spend time with people of different ages and situations.

The single person should have no fear of building friendships with a married couple, and vice versa. Such relationships can be fulfilling and helpful for both the single person and the family. Indeed, God has a special promise for lonely single people:

> *'God sets the lonely ____ ________________.'*
>
> (Psalm 68:6)

Claim what is rightfully yours!

In the church, support can be provided for widows and single-parent families. But the support given should strengthen the authority of the single parent rather than take over from it:

> *'Religion that God our Father accepts as pure and faultless is this: to ____________ ________________ ______________ and ____________ in their distress.'*
>
> (James 1:27).

Elderly people are never redundant in the Lord. They have much to give to younger people:

> *'Teach the __________ __________ to be reverent in the way they live, not to be slanderers or addicted to too much wine, but to teach what is good. Then they can __________ the ______________ __________ to love their husbands and children.'*
>
> (Titus 2:3-4)

When the very old and the very young are both secure in their situations they can be a shining example to the world of how, in the church, age differences need not be a barrier to relationship. God wants no 'generation gap' in his kingdom:

> *'Men and women of ripe old age will sit in the streets of Jerusalem, each with cane in hand because of his age. The city streets will be filled with boys and girls playing there.'*
>
> (Zechariah 8:4-5)

The secure person is always a great encourager. Let us avoid negative, critical and cynical attitudes and comments. Instead, let us do our utmost to enhance the security, development and ministry of others:

> *'____________________ one another and __________ ________ __________ ____, just as in fact you are doing.'*
>
> (1 Thessalonians 5:11)

4. Work

Our daily work is a relationship affair, whether it is working in an office or factory or being a homemaker. Frustrations can easily creep in when we feel disgruntled about our job, the people we work with, a lack of prospects, an inadequate salary – or not having a job at all.

If we have a job, let us be grateful for it and maintain a right attitude towards our employer and the level of income he sees fit to pay us. It is possible to ask for a pay rise firmly yet graciously if we think that is in order – provided we work diligently.

If we are in a position of oversight towards other workers, we should be secure in it without being overbearing, and ensure that they are receiving a salary worthy of the work they are doing:

> *'The worker deserves his wages.'*
>
> (Luke 10:7)

If we have no job satisfaction, either because we are out of work or because we are unhappy in our work environment, our security in God and the encouragement of others will make it possible to remain in faith either for a job or for better prospects. Rest in God. Anxious attempts to build your own security by greedy salary-seeking will lead to frustration and ultimate *in*security.

In every church there are people with aspirations to become 'full time' for God in the sense of being employed by the church in some capacity. We must not allow frustration to cause us to move ahead of our time; remember that it was several years after David had been anointed that he was actually proclaimed king.

If you sense God's call to ministry, be patient and allow him to work it out for you at the right time. Church leaders need wisdom to recognise the right timing for men and women to be released into full-time ministry.

But whatever our job, there is a sense in which we are all 'full-time' for God. Secular employment will be for most wage-earners the place where they are called to glorify him. If that was true of slaves in Paul's day, how much more so of us in our job situations:

> *'Slaves, obey your earthly masters with ________ and fear, and with sincerity of heart, just as you would ________ ________. Obey them not only to win their favour when their eye is on you, but like slaves of Christ, doing the ________ ____ ______ from your heart. Serve ____________________, as if you were serving the Lord, not men, because you know that the Lord will reward everyone for whatever good he does, whether he is slave or free.'*
>
> (Ephesians 6:5-8)

5. Covenant Relationships

In Jesus, God brought us into the new covenant – a relationship-agreement not only with himself but also with the body of Christ, our fellow-Christians. Covenant friendship involves:

a. Freedom to make friends

The best friendships are to be found among God's people, where there is a level of appreciation and trust unknown outside. Seek out one or more Christian friends with whom you can share and in whom you can confide.

Jealousy causes division between friends and spoils people's lives. If your friend gets on well with someone you don't know, be happy for him or her to have other good friendships apart from yours. It is good, in any case, to avoid cliques being formed within the church.

So while we have friendships, we must be secure enough in them to allow each other to have wider relationships, perhaps especially with non-Christians and with new people coming into the church.

b. Resolving difficulties

If someone offends you, be secure enough to talk with him or her in order to clear up any misunderstandings, mis-interpretations or thoughtlessness *immediately.* Things must not be left to fester, nor should insecurity persuade us to share our hurt with someone other than the person concerned:

> *'If your brother sins against you, go and show him his fault,* ***just between the two of you.*** *If he listens to you, you have won your brother over.'*
>
> (Matthew 18:15)

c. Different levels of friendship

It is impossible to have the same depth of relationship with everyone in the church. Jesus had varying levels of relationship with the multitudes that followed him, the seventy disciples he sent out and the twelve he called to be with him. Of the twelve disciples, he was more intimate with Peter, James and especially John, who was described as 'the disciple whom Jesus loved' (John 13:23). We, too, must be secure enough to maintain different levels of friendship.

In *all* our relationships we have clear guidelines from God's Word:

> *'Get rid of all bitterness, rage and anger, brawling and slander, along with every form of malice. Be ________ and __________________ to one another, _____________ each other, just as in Christ God forgave you.'*
>
> (Ephesians 4:31-32)

****

LESSON 5

Secure in Relationships

True or False

1. T F The fact that God wants to be recognised as our Father shows that he made no mistakes when he created us.

2. T F Being single is a problem that should cause the person concerned to feel ashamed.

3. T F It doesn't really matter how we talk to our children – as long as they get the message.

4. T F The secure person does his utmost to enhance the security, development and ministry of others in the church.

5. T F God wants us to glorify him in our daily work, whatever our job.

6. T F The best friendships are to be found among God's people.

7. T F Friendship means trying to ignore any misunderstanding, misinterpretation or thoughtlessness, however bad you feel inside.

8. T F We need to be secure enough to maintain different levels of friendship with people.

Group Discussion

1. Discuss the relationship of Jesus with his twelve disciples. Were they all secure in their relationships with him? What deepened their relationships?

2. In what environments do relationships best develop?

3. Why do some people find it easier than others to form close relationships? How can those who find it difficult be helped?

Personal Assignment

1. From the gospels, examine Jesus' relationship with three or four people, noting how they differed and how they were similar. What can you learn from them?

2. Try to give frank answers to the following questions:

    a. Do people only recognise me as Richard's wife (or Joan's husband)?

    b. Am I envious of the friendships others have? Do I often feel left out?

    c. Am I always trying to impress people?

    d. Am I looking for praise in what I do and say?

    e. Am I trying to conform to what I think people *expect* me to be?

    f. Am I constantly wondering what other people think of me?

    g. Do I try to hide my reactions from people?

    h. If someone corrects me, do I always try to justify myself?

    Each 'yes' answer indicates a need to find a deeper sense of personal security. Determine to work at those areas, with the Lord's help.

True or False

1.T 2.F 3.F 4.T 5.T 6.T 7.F 8.T

LESSON 6

Secure in God's Will

1. God's Will and the Renewed Mind

God's plan to fill the earth with his glory involves each of us. As we have seen, right from our conception he has been loving us. Now that we belong to him, he wants us to know his will for us – our personal part in his greater purpose.

> *'Do not conform any longer to the pattern of this world, but ______ ______________ by the ____________ of your ________. Then you will be able to test and approve what ________ ________ is – his ________, pleasing and ____________ will.'*
>
> (Romans 12:2)

God's will is good, says Paul. It is the best way for our lives, and with our renewed minds we are capable of embracing it. Discipline of our thought-life is necessary, because the wayward mind can cause us considerable insecurity. We need to apply our minds, with faith, to understanding God's great plan, so that we can joyfully embrace his will for our part in it.

Staying in the centre of God's will requires perseverance, but it brings satisfaction and a reward:

> *'You need to persevere so that when you have done the will of God, you will receive what he has promised.'*
>
> (Hebrews 10:36)

As we learn to trust God, our mind becomes steadfast and our thinking faithful. This results in mental stability for us concerning God's will:

> *'You will keep in perfect peace him whose mind is steadfast, because he trusts in you.'*
>
> (Isaiah 26:3)

2. God's Will is Simple

Many Christians become insecure about God's will and plan for their lives. They spend hours agonising before God over decisions, and in so doing assume that God doesn't want to make his will known to them! But it is a mistake to think that God's will is so mysterious that we can never be sure we have got it right.

God certainly has his plans for us, but they are not so permanently fixed that if we go slightly wrong we lose his presence, love and guidance. Confusion and doubt are not God's desire for his people. In his love for us he will always make things clear. Doubt comes from the enemy, so doubt your doubts!

> *'God is ______ a God of ______________ but of peace.'*
>
> (1 Corinthians 14:33)

Above all, God's will is *simple*. It is always clear and well-defined when we need specific direction. Notice that the Bible doesn't encourage us to 'seek' the will of God. It encourages us to 'do' his will, on the assumption that we know what it is. And our doing of it will always bring a sense of enjoyment and complete fulfilment. By his grace, we can say to God what Jesus said:

'I have come to do your will, O God.'

(Hebrews 10:7)

3. Doing God's Will

Scripture provides some practical guidelines which we can follow in pursuit of the will of God. Being spiritual doesn't mean being over-pious or heavenly-minded. Having given us a sound mind, God expects us to use it.

a. Holiness

Holiness of life is the general will of God for all his people, the background against which we sketch in the particulars:

'This is the will of God, that you should be holy.'

(1 Thessalonians 4:3 New English Bible)

All unrighteous acts automatically fall outside the will of God; in Christ we become 'the righteousness of God' (2 Corinthians 5:21). God therefore expects us to live and act in that righteousness.

b. Common sense

God provides us with common sense. He wants us to make sensible, commonsense decisions, and often that is a sufficient indicator of his will. For example, John the Baptist baptised in a part of the Jordan River where there was a lot of water – for obvious reasons (John 3:23)!

c. Divine intervention

Should God's will be opposed to our natural thinking, then he is able to intervene, as we shall see in the following examples:

1. Joseph made up his mind

During the period of Mary's engagement to Joseph, she came out with the devastating news that she was pregnant. And the explanation she gave was hardly reassuring to Joseph, who used his common sense in deciding what to do:

> *'He had in mind to divorce her quietly.'*
>
> (Matthew 1:19)

It was a sensible decision. He didn't wish to cause an uproar, but neither did he wish to ignore what had happened. So he didn't hesitate – he decided.

Once Joseph had made up his mind, the will of God could be implemented. And since in this instance his decision was the wrong one, God intervened. An angel of the Lord appeared to him in a dream and said:

> *'Joseph son of David, do not be afraid to take Mary home as your wife, because what is conceived in her is from the Holy Spirit.'*
>
> (Matthew 1:20).

When we are vacillating over which decision to make, God simply wants us to make up our minds one way or the other. The rest we can safely leave to him.

2. Paul decided to go

We tend to assume that the apostle Paul was a perfect man who always knew God's will and never got it wrong. This is a mistaken view.

On one occasion he decided to go to Asia with the gospel but ended up elsewhere, 'having been kept by the Holy Spirit from preaching the word in the province of Asia' (Acts 16:6). We would normally assume that the Holy Spirit would want any apostle to preach the gospel anywhere in the world, Asia included, but on this occasion God had his reasons for intervening and sending Paul instead to Phrygia and Galatia.

A similar thing happened when Paul and his companions tried to go into Bithynia:

> *'The Spirit of Jesus would not allow them to.'*
>
> (Acts 16:7)

Whether they were turned back by circumstances or prophetic direction we are not told. Either way, they took it to be the leading of the Holy Spirit.

These two instances, happening as they did immediately after each other, could have made Paul insecure about his guidance. He could have wondered whether he had been right in undertaking this apostolic journey in the first place, and maybe even toyed with the idea of returning to his home base at Antioch.

In fact, Paul did none of these things, because not only did the Holy Spirit step in when he had got it wrong, but the same Holy Spirit gave the apostle his new direction:

'During the night Paul had a ___________ of a man of Macedonia standing and begging him, "Come over to Macedonia and ________ ____." After Paul had seen the vision, we ______ __________ at once to leave for Macedonia, concluding that ______ ______ ____________ ____ to preach the gospel to them.'

(Acts 16:9-10)

4. Receiving Direction

God, who directed Joseph and Paul, will also give clear direction about his plans and his will for us. How?

a. God's Word

God's Word 'stands for ever' (Isaiah 40:8). Through it we can know guidance from God as to how to react and what to do in every situation. And *because* it is his Word, we should never entertain potential decisions which are contrary to the heart and purpose of God as expressed in the Bible.

When an expert in the law once came to Jesus and asked, 'What must I do to inherit eternal life?' (Luke 10:25), Jesus' reply turned him to the written Word of God:

' "What is written in the Law?" he replied. "How do you read it?" '

(Luke 10:26)

We can be secure in knowing that the written Word of God is unchanging and irrefutable. It is not just a book containing inspired words; it *is* the inspired Word of God and carries God's authority (see 2 Timothy 3:16-17). Read Psalm 119 to see the reverence shown by the psalmist for God's written law as a means of life-guidance.

b. Fellowship with God

Quite apart from the Bible, God wants to communicate with us personally. Through our intimate prayer-times with him he can speak to us, giving specific direction when necessary:

> *'Just as you received Christ Jesus as Lord, ___________ ____ _________ ____ _______, rooted and built up in him, strengthened in the faith as you were taught, and overflowing with thankfulness.'*
>
> (Colossians 2:6-7)

Although we may not audibly hear God, our intimacy with him and our openness of heart towards him give him the freedom to communicate through dreams, visions and angels, as he did in New Testament days (for example, Joseph and Paul in Section 3c above. See also Acts 2:17; 9:9-16; 12:6-10; 18:9-11). And none of these interventions will ever contravene his written Word.

c. Fellowship with God's people

We saw earlier that God does not intend us to be isolated from other Christians. One reason is that he can speak to us through them. And it isn't just that church members hear God through their leaders; it can work the other way round. For example, when Moses had put himself under too much pressure in settling the people's disputes, his father-in-law, Jethro, became God's mouthpiece for giving him some wise counsel about delegating authority. Although Moses was the leader, he responded to what Jethro said:

> *'Moses listened to his father-in-law and did ____________________ ____ ________.'*
>
> (Exodus 18:24)

As for David, he was the king, but he still needed to hear the voice of the prophet Nathan and repent of his sin concerning Bathsheba (2 Samuel 12:1-13).

Our close relationship with other Christians, and our open fellowship with them, will make us ready to hear the counsel of God through them. None of us has a monopoly of hearing God. If the king can listen to the prophet, and the leader of the people listen to his father-in-law, how much more do we need to hear the voice of God through his people – and not least through those whom he has chosen to lead us!

5. When God Intervenes

If God does intervene in your life in some dramatic way, remain secure. God's intervention hasn't come to threaten your confidence; he loves you, and it is for your good and the good of his people.

Don't be afraid of making mistakes; we all make them. But if we do make wrong decisions, God's intervention will redirect us and keep us secure in his presence. Also, our keeping close to him will enable us to distinguish between divine intervention and the circumstantial red herrings that Satan may draw across our path.

True security in God will enable us to receive his intervention in the right way. If God sends someone to speak to us, we must be open to receive that person as a messenger from God, bringing his loving counsel to us.

> *'Many are the plans in a man's heart, but it is the Lord's purpose that prevails.'*
>
> (Proverbs 19:21)

****

LESSON 6

Secure in God's Will

True or False

1. T F The will of God is very complicated.

2. T F The Bible says very little about *seeking* the will of God but plenty about *doing* it.

3. T F God wants us to make sensible, commonsense decisions – and if they are wrong he can then show us the right way.

4. T F Because the Word of God is unchanging, we should never entertain potential decisions which are contrary to God's heart and purpose as expressed in it.

5. T F Since they are unique, God-given dreams and visions frequently contravene the Bible.

6. T F I have my own personal relationship with God. Therefore, I don't need anyone else to advise me.

7. T F If I happen to miss the way, God's intervention will redirect me and keep me secure in his presence.

Group Discussion

1. Share personal testimonies of ways in which God has led you. Note the variety and consistency of the leading of God in these.

2. Discuss the situation mentioned about Joseph and Mary in Section 3c (Matthew 1:18-25). How would you have reacted in this situation? What can you learn from this?

Personal Assignment

1. List the crucial times in your life when you have known definite leading from God. How did God reveal his way to you?

2. Choose six people (three from the Old Testament, three from the New Testament) and observe how they knew the will of God. Underline or mark key words in each reference in your Bible.

3. Seek out another Christian and ask him how he knew it was the will of God for him to move to your town, change his job or get married. Share your experiences with him and note the consistency, yet individuality, with which God speaks.

True or False

1.F 2.T 3.T 4.T 5.F 6.F 7.T

Secure Under Attack

While some people regard Satan as a figment of the imagination, many Christians go to the other extreme and live in morbid fear of what this enemy of theirs may do. Some even seem to enjoy talking about Satan, demons and the occult.

There is danger in both extremes. We need to examine this subject to find a biblical balance and see how the Christian can retain his security in God against Satan, the enemy.

1. Who Satan Is

Satan is real, a created being who, through his rebellion, fell from his position as God's servant and instead became his enemy (see Isaiah 14:12-15). An understanding of the kind of person Satan is will help us to recognise some of the ways in which he will try to attack the people of God. We need that understanding:

> *'. . . in order that Satan might not __________ us. For we are not __________ of his __________.'*
>
> (2 Corinthians 2:11)

Satan's methods of attack include:

a. Accusation

Satan is known as 'the accuser of our brothers' (Revelation 12:10). He tries to rob the Christian of joy and security by bringing accusations against him. But God does not accuse us, neither does he condemn us. His Word assures us that:

> *'There is now* ***no condemnation*** *for those who are in Christ Jesus.'*
>
> (Romans 8:1)

So if you are feeling condemned, you know where it is coming from!

b. Lies

Jesus said about Satan:

> *'He was a murderer from the beginning, not holding to the truth, for there is ____ __________ in him. When he ______, he speaks his ________ ________, for he is a liar and the father of lies.'*
>
> (John 8:44)

In Eden, God warned Adam and Eve that if they ate the forbidden fruit they would die (Genesis 3:3). Satan's immediate response was, 'You will *not* surely die' (v4). He has been contradicting God's Word ever since. He will tell you, for example, that:

☐ You are no good

☐ You have nothing to contribute in the church

☐ You will never change

☐ Your sins are too serious to be forgiven

These are all lies! Find Bible verses which declare the very opposite.

c. Deception

Satan is clever, a subtle deceiver. He is never what he appears to be – in Eden he disguised himself as a serpent. He also uses people, and the Bible frequently warns us against deceitful people (for example, Ephesians 5:6; 2 Thessalonians 2:3). Paul warned the Corinthians about:

> '. . . *false apostles, deceitful workmen, masquerading as apostles of Christ. And no wonder, for Satan himself masquerades as an angel of light. It is not surprising, then, if his servants masquerade as servants of righteousness*'.
>
> (2 Corinthians 11:13-15)

Satan tries to infiltrate the people of God by sending in ferocious wolves in sheep's clothing (Matthew 7:15). But they can always be detected by Christians who live by the Spirit. Be secure in that. They give themselves away by their attempts to destroy people's faith and by their lack of abundant life and good character.

2. The Extent of His Power

Satan's power, though great, is limited. Being a created being, his power is less than the power of the Creator – who is also your loving, heavenly Father! And the Holy Spirit within us gives us the upper hand:

> *'You, dear children, are from God and have overcome them, because the one who is _____ _______ is ____________ than the one who is ____ _____ _________.'*
>
> (1 John 4:4)

And we don't have to be elderly, experienced Christians for this to be true. It was to young men that John wrote: 'You have overcome the evil one' (1 John 2:14).

Satan may have authority in the world today, but he has no authority over us, as God's people:

> *'We know that we are children of God, and that the whole world is under the control of the evil one.'*
>
> (1 John 5:19)

Satan is limited not only in his immediate power but also in the amount of time he has left before his ultimate destruction (Revelation 20:10).

Rest secure in the fact that God is in total control; the Spirit-filled believer can be sure that 'the evil one cannot harm him' (1 John 5:18). Don't let anyone convince you otherwise!

3. Satan and Your Salvation

Our salvation is secure, because it is God's doing, not our own

(1 Corinthians 1:30). It is founded upon a rock and cannot be shaken (Matthew 7:24-27).

Satan cannot take it away from us – but he will try to convince us he can! He will plant seeds of doubt in our minds which, if we allow them to remain, will germinate and grow until we start to believe the doubts rather than the truth. We should tune in instead to the voice of Jesus, who said:

> *'My sheep listen to my voice; I know them, and they follow me. I give them eternal life, and they shall never perish; no-one can snatch them out of my hand. My Father, who has given them to me, is greater than all; no-one can snatch them out of my Father's hand.'*
>
> (John 10:27-29)

If Satan cannot convince us of the invalidity of our salvation, he may well try to confuse us with strange doctrines. For example, he knows, only too well, that Jesus died on the cross and that he actually rose physically from the dead, but if he can persuade us to doubt these truths he will weaken our security in God.

4. A Tool in God's Hand

Satan always fails to thwart the plans and purpose of God in Jesus, because in his attempts he actually ends up fulfilling what God had designed. The Bible tells us that it was Satan's entering into Judas that prompted him to betray Jesus (Luke 22:3-4). But when Jesus was subsequently crucified, it wasn't Satan's masterstroke, but God's. It became the source of our salvation! (See Acts 2:23.)

God is able to do the same kind of thing for us. He will turn Satan's tricks to his own advantage – and to ours.

The apostle Paul was able to learn and grow as a direct result of satanic attack. While being blessed with 'surpassingly great revelations' from God, he suffered what he described as 'a thorn in my flesh, a messenger of Satan, to torment me' (2 Corinthians 12:7). Not wishing to suffer any longer than necessary, he asked God to remove it. But, instead, God used the pressure of the situation to strengthen Paul and teach him about grace. His words to Paul were:

> *'My grace is sufficient for you, for my power is made perfect in weakness.'*
>
> (2 Corinthians 12:9)

Paul didn't become depressed. He didn't think that he had lost God's love or that he was lacking in faith. He saw instead that God was offering him the chance to become a better servant, and with faith and confidence he seized the opportunity:

> *'I will boast all the more gladly about my weaknesses, so that ______________ ___________ may rest on me. That is why, for Christ's sake, I delight in weaknesses, in insults, in hardships, in persecutions, in difficulties. For when I am ________, then I am ____________.'*
>
> (2 Corinthians 12:9-10)

This wasn't mere positive thinking; it was using faith to grasp God's opportunities. If God ever deals with us like that, we can adopt the same faithful and confident attitude, knowing that 'in all things God works for the good of those who love him, who have been called according to his purpose' (Romans 8:28).

God's faithfulness towards us will always prove greater than any enemy attack; he will see us through:

> *'No temptation has seized you except what is common to man. And ______ ____ ______________ ; he will not let you be tempted beyond what you can bear. But when you are tempted, he will also ______________ __ ______ ______ so that you can stand up under it.'*
>
> (1 Corinthians 10:13)

Don't make the mistake of allowing your attention to focus on Satan when he attacks. Focus on our faithful, sustaining God, and on him alone.

5. How He Attacks

Satan is crafty and subtle. He normally attacks at our weak points. Rarely will he knock at the front door and ask us to let him in! Rather, he will sneak in by a back way and take us unawares with his questioning:

- ☐ 'Did God say . . . ?'
- ☐ 'Is it really true?'
- ☐ 'How can you be sure?'

He begins, not by directly contradicting what God has said – that would be too obvious – but by undermining our faith, to produce doubt in our minds. The mind is the main target of his attacks. Read Luke 4:1-13 and study how he tempted Jesus in the wilderness.

Guard your mind! It is easy to give place to faithless and even illogical thoughts about God and about other Christians. Satan might suggest that nobody cares about us. Or he might sow a thought in our mind which, if dwelt on, will result in our alienation from the security and blessing of fellowship.

We might overhear part of a conversation and get a mistaken impression. Or a well-meaning friend might say something which makes us fearful. Let us determine not to be swayed by hearsay. As God's faithful people, all our thinking should be righteous.

Above all else, Satan wishes to make us insecure and he will try all means to achieve this end. We must therefore learn to recognise the signs of Satan's attack, and be ready to take action against it.

6. Resisting Him

> *'Resist the devil, and he will flee from you. Come near to God and he will come near to you.'*
>
> (James 4:7-8)

How do we resist Satan? Since he attacks us mainly in the mind, it is the realm of the mind which needs to come under the discipline of the Holy Spirit and the Word of God. It is our own responsibility to keep our minds in purity:

> '______ ________ ________ *on things above, not on earthly things.'*
>
> (Colossians 3:2)

We can defeat Satan totally in the area of the mind by taking firm and decisive action against wrong thoughts before they have a chance to ensnare us:

> *'We demolish arguments and every pretension that sets itself up against the knowledge of God, and we ________ ____________ __________ ____________ to make it obedient to Christ.'*
>
> (2 Corinthians 10:5)

We should never try to empty our mind and think of nothing, because it is the empty house that Satan can attempt to take over (Matthew 12:43-45). God encourages us to fill our minds with the truth of his Word and other good and wholesome thoughts:

> *'Whatever is true, whatever is noble, whatever is right, whatever is pure, whatever is lovely, whatever is admirable – if anything is excellent or praiseworthy – __________ __________ ________ _________.'*
>
> (Philippians 4:8)

Avoid dwelling on things that are miserable, violent, sickening or depressing. God is good, and he always makes sure we have plenty of good things to think about and sing about, such as the way he blesses and encourages us and gives us trustworthy families and friends:

> *'Let the word of Christ dwell in you richly as you teach and admonish one another with all wisdom, and as you sing psalms, hymns and spiritual songs with gratitude in your hearts to God.'*
>
> (Colossians 3:16)

By our obedience to the Word of God and by being continually filled with the Spirit, we are not only resisting Satan; we are making it difficult for him to attack us in the first place!

7. A Defeated Foe

Satan has already been defeated (Colossians 2:15; Luke 10:18-19). The cross, resurrection and ascension of Jesus made sure that the devil had no more hope and that he would be under the sentence of death until the end of time.

God knows that Satan is defeated. Satan himself knows it (Revelation 12:12) – and so do we. He is limited in every way. He is less powerful than we are, and he is heading for destruction. We will live for ever; Satan won't. We rule; Satan's kingdom is defeated. Jesus prayed:

> *'My prayer is not that you take them out of the world but that you protect them from the evil one.'*
>
> (John 17:15)

That prayer is guaranteed its answer. In the strength of it, rest secure!

LESSON 7

Secure Under Attack

True or False

1. T F While Satan is the 'accuser of the brothers', God does not accuse us or condemn us.
2. T F It is difficult for a Christian to detect Satan's ferocious wolves in sheep's clothing.
3. T F There is no limit to the devil's power and to the ways in which he can attack us.
4. T F Satan cannot take our salvation from us – but he will try to convince us he can.
5. T F Satan's attempts to thwart God's plan and purpose end up fulfilling what God designed.
6. T F The body, rather than the mind, is the main target of Satan's attacks.
7. T F God encourages us to fill our minds with the truth of his Word as well as with good and wholesome thoughts.
8. T F It isn't our responsibility to resist evil thoughts.
9. T F We can rest secure in the fact that God will protect us from the evil one.

Group Discussion

1. Paul says that we are aware of Satan's schemes. Talk about some of the patterns of pressure and temptations you have observed, and how you have learnt to counter them.

2. Why does Satan usually tempt us with something which seems small and innocuous to begin with? Why is it important to deal with these temptations promptly and effectively?

3. Discuss practical ways to develop a disciplined, godly thought life. Encourage one another to be holy, living lives glorifying to God; thinking wholesome thoughts; speaking edifying words.

Personal Assignment

1. What positive steps can you take to protect yourself from evil thoughts? Determine to take a more positive approach to thinking.

2. Collect together some key Bible verses which you can use against the enemy when under various kinds of attack. Learn them by heart.

3. Spend time in personal praise to God for the increased security you have found in him as a result of working through this series of studies.

True or False

1.T 2.F 3.F 4.T 5.T 6.F 7.T 8.F 9.T